Anglican Foundations Series 07

Instruction in the Way of the Lord

A Guide to the Catechism in the Book of Common Prayer

by Martin Davie

The Latimer Trust

Instruction in the Way of the Lord: A Guide to the Catechism in the Book of Common Prayer © Martin Davie 2014

ISBN   978-1-906327-25-5

Cover photo: Wisteria, Wales, UK© TAGSTOCK3- fotolia.com

Scripture quotations are from the Revised Standard Version of the Bible, copyright © 1946, 1952, and 1971 the Division of Christian Education of the National Council of the Churches of Christ in the United States of America. Used by permission. All rights reserved.

Published by the Latimer Trust October 2014

The Latimer Trust (formerly Latimer House, Oxford) is a conservative Evangelical research organisation within the Church of England, whose main aim is to promote the history and theology of Anglicanism as understood by those in the Reformed tradition. Interested readers are welcome to consult its website for further details of its many activities.

The Latimer Trust
London N14 4PS UK
Registered Charity: 1084337
Company Number: 4104465
Web: www.latimertrust.org
E-mail: administrator@latimertrust.org

Views expressed in works published by The Latimer Trust are those of the authors and do not necessarily represent the official position of The Latimer Trust.

Foreword to the Anglican Foundations Series

The recent celebration of the 350th anniversary of the 1662 *Book of Common Prayer* has helped to stimulate a renewed interest in its teaching and fundamental contribution to Anglican identity. Archbishop Cranmer and others involved in the English Reformation knew well that the content and shape of the services set out in the Prayer Book were vital ways of teaching congregations biblical truth and the principles of the Christian gospel. This basic idea of '*lex orandi, lex credendi*' is extremely important. For good or ill, the content and shape of our meetings as Christians is highly influential in shaping our practice in following the Lord Jesus Christ.

Furthermore, increased interest in the historic formularies of the Church of England has been generated by the current painful divisions within the Anglican Communion which inevitably highlight the matter of Anglican identity. In the end our Anglican Foundations cannot be avoided since our identity as Anglicans is intimately related to the question of Christian identity, and Christian identity cannot avoid questions of Christian understanding and belief. While the 39 Articles often become the focus of discussions about Christian and Anglican belief (and have been addressed in this series through *The Faith We Confess* by Gerald Bray) the fact that the 1662 *Book of Common Prayer* and the Ordinal are also part of the doctrinal foundations of the Church of England is often neglected.

Thus the aim of this series of booklets which focus on the Formularies of the Church of England and the elements of the different services within the Prayer Book is to highlight what those services teach about the Christian faith and to demonstrate how they are also designed to shape the practice of that faith. As well as providing an account of the origins of the Prayer Book services, these booklets are designed to offer practical guidance on how such services may be used in Christian ministry nowadays.

It is not necessary to use the exact 1662 services in order to be true to our Anglican heritage, identity and formularies. However if we grasp the principles of Cranmer which underpinned those services then modern versions of them can fulfil the same task of teaching congregations how to live as Christians which Cranmer intended. If we are ignorant of the principles of Cranmer then our Sunday gatherings will inevitably teach something to Anglican congregations, but it will not be the robust biblical faith which Cranmer promoted.

So our hope is that through this Anglican Foundations series our identity as Anglicans will be clarified and that there will be by God's grace a renewal of the teaching and practice of the Christian faith through the services of the Church of England and elsewhere within the Anglican Communion.

Mark Burkill and Gerald Bray

Series Editors, The Latimer Trust

CONTENTS

1	How the Catechism fits into the *Book of Common Prayer*	1
2	The History of the Catechism	10
2.1	*The background and development of the Catechism*	10
2.2	*The Authorship of the Catechism*	15
3	The Structure of the Catechism	18
4	The Teaching of the Catechism	20
4.1	*The Christian Covenant*	20
4.2	*The Apostles Creed*	23
4.3	*The Ten Commandments*	27
4.4	*The Lord's Prayer*	31
4.5	*The Sacraments*	35
5	The continuing value of the Catechism	40
Appendix A	The Catechism of 1549	43
Appendix B	Alternative Anglican catechetical material	47
	The Revised Catechism (1962)	47
	Pilgrim	48
	To be a Christian	49
Appendix C	The social significance of the teaching of the Catechism about our duty towards our neighbour	50

1 How the Catechism fits into the *Book of Common Prayer*

In the *Book of Common Prayer* the Catechism comes between the three orders of service for Baptism and the order for Confirmation. This position reflects the fact that the function of the Catechism is to provide an educational bridge between infant baptism and confirmation.

The English Reformers inherited a pattern of Christian initiation involving confirmation which developed in the Western Church from the end of the Patristic period onwards.

In the fourth and fifth centuries, while there was no single agreed rite of Christian initiation, there was, in the Western Church at least, a broadly similar overall pattern of Christian initiation with many common elements. This pattern involved a period of catechetical instruction followed by testing, prayer and fasting. There was then a vigil, sometimes night long, at the cathedral church. This vigil normally took place on Holy Saturday or the Eve of Pentecost, and occasionally at other times. Following the vigil the candidates renounced evil, and made a profession of faith. They were then baptised in water in the name of the Trinity by the presbyters assisted by the deacons.

In some places there were anointings by a presbyter after the baptism and the candidates were taken to the bishop who completed the rite with a prayer for the sevenfold gifts of the Spirit listed in Isaiah 11:2 accompanied by the laying on of hands and/or anointing with the oil of chrism.

In the fourth and fifth centuries 'Baptism' was a short-hand way of referring to all the various elements of this rite.[1] What we would call confirmation was thus part of baptism. From the fifth century onwards, however, three developments took place which led to the dissolution of this single complex rite of initiation, at least in the Western church.

First, infant baptism became the norm. This meant that the traditional pattern of catechesis prior to baptism and personal confession of faith at baptism ceased in the case of most of those who

---

[1] For a convenient compilation of the documentary evidence for the baptismal rites in the Patristic period see E. C. Whitaker, and M.E. Johnson, *Documents of the Baptismal Liturgy*, 3rd ed, (Collegeville: Liturgical Press, 2003).

were being baptised. The pattern that replaced it was one in which the personal confession of faith and commitment at baptism was undertaken by parents and Godparents on behalf of infants on the understanding that these infants would receive catechetical instruction as they grew up and confess the faith for themselves.

Secondly, the direct link between baptism and admission to communion was broken. Admission to Holy Communion was postponed until infants who had been baptised were old enough to receive the sacrament with a proper degree of understanding.

Thirdly, the growth of the Church in Western Europe from the fifth to the eleventh centuries and the large size of many Western dioceses, particularly north of the Alps, meant that it became impractical for a bishop to preside over all the baptismal rites in person.

As a result of these three factors the final part of the Western baptismal rite, the laying on of hands with prayer by the bishop, eventually became a separate rite. In the Western Church in the Middle Ages there were thus two rites of Christian initiation. The first was Baptism, normally presided over by a priest, and the second was Confirmation, which was presided over by the bishop. The role of the bishops was justified by reference to the action of the Apostles in Acts 8:4-7, the bishops being understood as the descendants of the Apostles in this regard.

The existence of a separate rite of Confirmation raised the question of the meaning of this second rite and the dominant Medieval understanding of this issue reflected the idea attributed to Faustus of Riez, a fifth century Gallic bishop, that the laying on of hands following Baptism strengthened people to live out the Christian life. A Pentecost sermon commonly attributed to Faustus states:

> The Holy Spirit who descends upon the waters of baptism by a salvific falling, bestows on the font a fullness towards innocence, and presents in confirmation an increase of grace. And because in this world we who will be prevailing must walk in every age between invisible enemies and dangers, we are reborn in baptism for life, and we are confirmed after baptism for the strife. In baptism we are washed, after baptism we are strengthened. And although the benefits of rebirth suffice immediately for those about to die, nevertheless the helps of confirmation are necessary for those who will prevail. Rebirth itself immediately saves those needing to be received in the peace of the blessed age. Confirmation arms and

supplies those needing to be preserved for the struggles and battles of this world. But the one who arrives at death after baptism, unstained with acquired innocence is confirmed by death because one can no longer sin after death.[2]

Although this sermon is in fact expounding the significance of the different parts of a still unified baptismal rite it came to be understood as referring to the two rites of Baptism and Confirmation, and on the basis of an alternative attribution to the fourth century Pope Militiades, it was included in Gratian's *Decretum* (c. 1140) which became an important source for Western Canon law.

Because Confirmation had become a chronologically separate rite from baptism, with a theological significance of its own, it came to be regarded in the Middle Ages as a distinct sacrament. There were thus two complementary sacraments of Christian initiation, Baptism and Confirmation.

In 1439, The Council of Florence ruled that 'there are seven sacraments of the New Law, viz, baptism, confirmation, the eucharist, penance, extreme unction, orders and marriage.' It went on to say that 'through baptism we are spiritually reborn; through confirmation we grow in grace and are strengthened in faith.'[3]

Although children were confirmed in infancy, there was a trend in the Middle Ages towards deferring the rite to a later age. This was partly because bishops were not readily available and because Confirmation was not viewed as necessary for salvation in the way that Baptism was. Eventually, the normal age of Confirmation was fixed at seven years old, but the practice of confirming younger infants when a bishop was available persisted throughout the Middle Ages. For example, in 1533 The future Queen Elizabeth I was baptised and confirmed when she was only three days old, because a bishop was readily available at the royal court.

During the Middle Ages there was a continuing debate about the relationship between the three sacraments of Baptism, Confirmation and Holy Communion. It was accepted, in line with Christian practice

---

[2] Text in P.Turner, *Sources of Confirmation, from the Fathers through the Reformation*, (Collegeville: The Liturgical Press, 1993), pp 35-36.
[3] Texts in J.H. Leith, *Creeds of the Churches*, rev ed., (Oxford: Basil Blackwell, 1973), pp 60-61.

from the earliest times, that Baptism had to precede admission to Holy Communion, but there was discussion about whether Confirmation had to precede Holy Communion as well.

In England Archbishop John Peckham decreed at the Council of Lambeth in 1281 that no-one should be admitted to Communion before he or she was confirmed. This regulation seems to have been aimed at bolstering confirmation by giving people an incentive to have their children confirmed. In line with this regulation the rubric of the Manual of the *Sarum Rite* declared that 'no one must be admitted to the sacrament of the body and blood of Christ save in danger of death, unless he has been confirmed or has been reasonably prevented from receiving the sacrament of confirmation' [4]

The Church of England of the sixteenth and seventeenth centuries retained a number of elements of the theology and practice of confirmation that had been developed in the Western Church during the Medieval Period:

- The existence of a rite of confirmation that was separate from the rite of baptism;
- The idea of Confirmation as strengthening believers. Archbishop Cranmer's first confirmation rite of 1549 used the words 'send down...thy Holy Ghost', but in 1552 he changed this to 'strengthen them... with the Holy Ghost' and it was the 1552 language that was used in the definitive 1662 version of the *Book of Common Prayer*;
- The practice of baptism being performed by a priest and confirmation being performed by a bishop;
- The medieval English discipline of insisting that confirmation should be the normal pre-requisite to receiving Holy Communion.

However, it also departed from medieval theology and practice in three key ways.

First, the Church of England rejected the idea that confirmation should be considered a sacrament. In the words of Article XXV:

---

[4] G Cameron, 'The Development of Confirmation and its relationship to Admission to Communion' in J Conn, N Doe and J Fox (eds), *Initiation, Membership and Authority in Anglican and Roman Catholic Canon Law* (Cardiff and Rome: The Centre for Law and Religion Cardiff University/ Pontifical Gregorian University/ Pontifical University of St.Thomas Aquinas), p 74.

> 'There are two Sacraments ordained of Christ our Lord in the Gospel, that is to say, Baptism and the Supper of the Lord.
>
> Those five commonly called Sacraments, that is to say, Confirmation, Penance, Orders, Matrimony, and Extreme Unction, are not to be counted for Sacraments of the Gospel, being such as have grown partly of the corrupt following of the Apostles, partly are states of life allowed in the Scriptures; but yet have not the like nature of Sacraments with Baptism and the Lord's Supper, for that they have not any visible sign or ceremony ordained of God.'

The Anglican Reformers believed that there was no evidence in the New Testament that confirmation had been instituted by Christ himself and they felt that the idea that it was a sacrament had led to an undervaluing of the importance of baptism. As the Elizabethan Dean of St. Paul's, Alexander Nowell, put it, the theologians of the Middle Ages had invented the idea of a sacrament of confirmation and:

> This invention of theirs they would needs have to be a sacrament, and accounted it in manner equal in dignity with baptism; yea, some of them preferred it also before baptism. By all means they would that this their confirmation should be taken for a certain supplying of baptism, that it should thereby be finished and brought to perfection, as though baptism else were unperfect, and as though children who in baptism had put upon them Christ with his benefits, without their confirmation were but half Christians; than which injury no greater could be done against the divine sacrament, and against God himself, and Christ our saviour, the author and founder of the holy sacrament of baptism.[5]

Secondly, the Church of England omitted some elements of the medieval confirmation rite. In the 1549 Prayer Book the use of the oil of chrism at confirmation was discontinued and the 1552 Prayer Book talked about the bishop laying his hand on the head of the person being confirmed without mentioning signing with the cross (although signing with the cross continued and was the form that the laying on of hands took in some places).

Thirdly, a new catechetical element was introduced into Church of England confirmations. As we shall see in the next chapter, the medieval Church had sought to ensure that children who were baptised

---

[5] G E Corrie (ed) *Nowell's Catechism*, (Cambridge: Parker Society/CUP, 1843), p 211.

would be brought up to know at least the basic elements of the Christian faith including the Lord's Prayer, the Ten Commandments and the Creed, but children did not answer for themselves at confirmation. The English Reformers however, like their Continental counterparts, believed that in the Early Church those baptised as infants were catechized before being brought to a bishop for Confirmation and sought to restore this early practice. Patristic scholars today do not believe that the catechesis of those baptised as infants was practised in the Early Church, but that is what the English Reformers believed to have been the case.

We can see this if we turn again to Nowell. He gives the following account of the practice of the Early Church (in it, S stands for scholar and M for master):

> S. Parents and Schoolmasters did in old times diligently instruct their children, as soon as by age they were able to perceive and understand, in the first principles of Christian religion, that they might suckle in godliness almost with the nurse's milk and straightways after their cradle might be nourished with the tender fruit of virtue towards that blessed life. For the which purpose also little short books, which we name Catechisms were written, wherein the same, or very like, matters as we are now in hand with, were entreated upon. And after that the children seemed to be sufficiently trained in the principles of our religion, they brought and offered them to the bishop.
>
> M. For what purpose did they so?
>
> S. That children might after baptism do the same which such as were older, who were also called *catechumeni*, that is, scholars of religion, did in old time before, or rather, at baptism itself. For the bishop did require and the children did render reason and account of their religion and faith: and such children as the bishop judged to have sufficiently profited in the understanding of religion he allowed, and laying his hands upon them, and blessing them, let them depart. This allowance and blessing of the bishop our men do call Confirmation.[6]

---

[6] Corrie (ed) *Nowell's Catechism*, pp 210-11.

Nowell went on to explain that it would be a good idea if this practice of the Early Church were to be restored as a way of tackling the problems afflicting the Christian faith in Tudor England:

> M. It were to be wished therefore that the ancient manner and usage of examining children were restored again?
>
> S. Very much to be wished. For so should godly parents be brought to the satisfying of their duty in godly bringing up of their children, which they now for the most part do leave undone, and quite reject from them; which part of their duty if parents or schoolmasters would take in hand, do, and thoroughly perform, there would be a marvellous consent and agreement in religion and faith, which is now in miserable sort torn asunder; surely all should not either lie so shadowed and overwhelmed with darkness and ignorance, or with dissension of divers and contrary opinions be so dissolved, disturbed and dissipated, as it is to this day: the more pity it is, and most to be most to be sorrowed of all good men for so miserable a case.[7]

This understanding of the importance of the catechetical element in confirmation is reflected in the opening words of the confirmation service in the *Book of Common Prayer*. These words declare:

> To the end that Confirmation may be ministered to the more edifying of such as shall receive it, the Church hath thought good to order, That none hereafter shall be confirmed, but such as can say the Creed, the Lord's Prayer, and the Ten Commandments; and can also answer to such other Questions, as in the short Catechism are contained: which order is very convenient to be observed; to the end that children being now come to the years of discretion, and having learned what their Godfathers and Godmothers promised for them in Baptism, they may themselves, with their own mouth and consent, openly before the Church, ratify and confirm the same; and also promise, that by the grace of God they will evermore endeavour themselves faithfully to observe such things, as they by their own confession have assented unto.

The Church of England thus insisted that a knowledge of the contents of the Catechism was required of confirmation candidates so that they could give meaningful personal assent to the promises made for them

---

[7] Corrie (ed) *Nowell's Catechism*, pp 211-12.

by their Godparents at their baptism and commit themselves to living out these promises in the future.

The requirement that candidates for confirmation should have a knowledge of the Catechism and be able to answer for themselves meant that the age of confirmation was increased from seven to the early teens, since the emphasis was no longer on children receiving additional sacramental grace as soon as possible after Baptism, but on people coming to Confirmation only if they had sufficient knowledge and spiritual maturity to answer for themselves (that is what is meant by 'come to the years of discretion').

In order that candidates for confirmation should have a knowledge of the contents of the Catechism and so be able to answer for themselves an educational process was required. The outline of this is set out in the rubric at the end of the Catechism. This states:

> The Curate of every Parish shall diligently upon Sundays and Holydays, after the second Lesson at Evening Prayer, openly in the Church instruct and examine so many Children of his Parish sent unto him, as he shall think convenient, in some part of this Catechism.
>
> And all Fathers, Mothers, Masters, and Dames, shall cause their Children, Servants, and Prentices, (which have not learned their Catechism,) to come to the Church at the time appointed, and obediently to hear and be ordered by the Curate, until such time as they have learned all that is here appointed for them to learn.
>
> So soon as Children are come to a competent age, and can say, in their mother tongue, the Creed, the Lord's Prayer, and the Ten Commandments; and also can answer to the other questions of this short Catechism; they shall be brought to the Bishop: And every one shall have a Godfather, or a Godmother, as a witness of their Confirmation.
>
> And whensoever the Bishop shall give knowledge for Children to be brought unto him for their Confirmation, the Curate of every Parish shall either bring or send in writing, with his hand subscribed thereunto, the names of all such persons within his Parish, as he shall think fit to be presented to the Bishop to be confirmed. And, if the Bishop approve of them, he shall confirm them in

manner following.[8]

What is interesting to note is that what is envisaged here is that the Christian instruction of children and young people is not, as in our day, just the responsibility of the Church and of Christian parents and Godparents. In this rubric it is assumed that the whole community has a proper interest in, and responsibility for, supporting Godparents in ensuring that children and young people are educated in the Christian faith into which they were baptised.

It is also important to understand that the role of the Curate was not simply to ensure that the children and young people learned the contents of the Catechism by rote. They would have been expected to memorise the Catechism so that they could recite it if necessary, but the Curate would also have explained its meaning to them and pointed them to the biblical passages that underlay its teaching. We know this because of the numerous commentaries on the Catechism that were produced to help clergy to undertake this additional instruction.

What this examination of the place of the Catechism in the Prayer Book shows us is the seriousness with which the Church of England of the sixteenth and seventeenth centuries took the issue of the Christian nurture of its children. As Bishop Thomas Ken put it in his 1685 commentary on the Catechism: 'in good earnest, it is less cruel and unnatural to deny them bread for their mortal bodies, than saving knowledge for their immortal souls.' This being the case, he writes:

> I passionately exhort and beseech you all, of either sex, never to cease your conscientious zeal for their instruction, till you bring them to Confirmation; to renew their Baptismal Vow; to make an open Profession of their Christianity; to discharge their Godfathers and Godmother; to receive the solemn benediction of the Bishop, to share in the public intercessions of the Church, and to partake of all the graces of God's Holy Spirit, implored on their behalf; that God, who has begun (Philippians 1.6) a good work in them, may perfect it till the Day of Christ.[9]

---

[8] In this rubric 'Curate' means the priest who has the cure of souls for a particular parish. 'Dame' means what we would call female school teachers and 'Prentices' means those who have been apprenticed to someone to learn a trade.

[9] Thomas Ken, *The Practice of Divine Love*, (London: Rivington, 1741), The Epistle Dedicatory.

2 The History of the Catechism

2.1 *The background and development of the Catechism*

The Greek verb *katecheo*, from which our English words catechesis and catechism are derived, originally meant to inform someone about something in a general sense, but by New Testament times it had come to have the specific meaning of giving someone religious instruction. It is in this sense that it is used in the New Testament.[1]

Thus we read in Acts 18:25 that Apollos had been 'instructed in the way of the Lord' and in Romans 2:18 St. Paul writes about people who boast about their relationship with God because they have been 'instructed in the law.' The same word is used by St. Paul in 1 Corinthians 14:19: 'I would rather speak five words with my mind to instruct others, than ten thousand words in a tongue'; and Galatians 6:6: 'let him who is taught the word share all good things with him who teaches.'

In the Early Church catechesis came to be used to refer to the instruction given to new converts ('catechumens') in which they were taught the basic elements of the faith such as the Creed, the Lord's Prayer and the meaning of the sacraments in preparation for Baptism. During the fourth and fifth centuries the baptismal rite described in the previous chapter was preceded by a period of intensive catechetical preaching, often given by the bishop himself,[2] so that the candidates would understand the profession of faith they were making when they recited the Creed at the Easter vigil prior to their baptism.

Once infant baptism became the norm, the focus of catechesis changed to the instruction of those who had been baptised and the word 'catechism' came to be used for the manuals of instruction drawn up for this purpose, the 'little short books' referred to by Nowell.

From the earliest days of the English Church there was a recognition of the vital importance of catechetical instruction. Thus

---

[1] W Bauer, F Gingrich and F Danker, *A Greek-English Lexicon of the New Testament*, 2nd ed, (Chicago and London: Chicago University Press, 1979), p 423.
[2] See, for example, the Catechetical lectures of St. Cyril of Jerusalem, in *The Nicene and Post Nicene Fathers*, 2nd series, vol. VII, (Edinburgh and Grand Rapids, T&T Clark/Eerdmans, 1996).

Bede wrote to Archbishop Egbert of York in the early eighth century: 'I consider it above every other thing important, that you should endeavour to implant deeply in the memory of all men the Catholic faith which is contained in the Apostles' Creed, and the Lord's Prayer.'[3]

This concern with the importance of catechesis continued to be a feature of the life of the English Church and by the late Middle Ages there was a formal requirement that during the baptism service the Priest should admonish the Godparents to ensure that the child being baptised learned the Lord's Prayer, the Hail Mary and the Apostles Creed.[4]

The three elements of instruction just mentioned formed the core of a wider scheme of catechetical instruction which had been laid down by the Council of Lambeth in 1281. In the words of Eamon Duffy, the Council drew up a 'schema of instruction for the laity' which was to be:

> ...expounded in the vernacular to parishioners four times in the year. This scheme was structured round the Creed, the Ten Commandments and Christ's summary of these in the dual precept to love God and neighbour, the seven works of mercy, the seven virtues, the seven vices and seven sacraments, and was intended to provide a comprehensive guide to Christian belief and practice.[5]

This framework for religious instruction, known by its opening words as the *Ignorantia Sacerdotum*, became the basis for the catechetical activity of the English Church right up to the Reformation, being reissued by Cardinal Wolsey in 1518. Numerous manuals of instruction were produced based on this framework and they too continued to be published up until the Reformation. For example, Richard Whytford published *A Werke for Householders*, which was a manual of instruction for the laity based on this traditional framework, in 1530, four years before the breach with Rome.[6]

At the Reformation the English Reformers were therefore faced with the existence of a programme for religious instruction that was well established and well resourced, but which reflected the theology and practice of Medieval Catholicism, many parts of which they rejected as

---

[3] J. A. Giles *The Historical Works of the Venerable Bede*, Vol. II, (London, 1845), pp 138-155.
[4] E Duffy, *The Stripping of the Altars*, (London and New Haven, Yale, 1992), p 53.
[5] Duffy, *The Stripping of the Altars*, p 53.
[6] Duffy, *The Stripping of the Altars*, pp 86-87.

untrue to the teaching of the New Testament and the Early Church. As a result they needed a new authorised framework for basic religious instruction and the Catechism in *The Book of Common Prayer* was produced to meet this need in the same way that, for instance, Luther's *Small Catechism* of 1529 was drawn up to meet the need for religious instruction in the churches of Saxony.

A first move towards the production of the Catechism can be found in the injunctions to the Church issued by Henry VIII in 1538, which were written by Thomas Cromwell. These tell the clergy what they need to be doing to instruct the laity:

> ...you shall every Sunday and holy day through the year openly and plainly recite to your parishioners twice or thrice together, or oftener if need require, one particle or sentence of the Paternoster or Creed, in English, to the intent they may learn the same by heart, and so from day to day to give them one like lesson or sentence of the same, till they have learned the whole Paternoster or Creed, in English, by rote; and as they shall be taught every sentence of the same by rote, you shall expound and declare the understanding of the same unto them, exhorting all parents and householders to teach their children and servants the same, as they are bound in conscience to do, and that done, you shall declare unto them the Ten Commandments, one by one, every Sunday and holyday, till they be likewise perfect in the same.[7]

What we find here are the three basic elements that are subsequently found in the Catechism; instruction in the Lord's Prayer, the Creed and the Ten Commandments, together with a requirement for regular weekly instruction and a reminder of the need for children and servants to be taught the basics of the Christian faith. What is missing is any link between religious instruction and Confirmation and any authorised manual of instruction.

The injunctions issued by Edward VI in 1547 contain the same instructions as in 1538, but in a slightly condensed form.[8]

The *First Prayer Book* of 1549 contained the first version of the Catechism which formed part of the order of service for Confirmation

---

[7] The Second Henrician Injunctions, O4, in G Bray (ed) *Documents of the English Reformation*, (Cambridge: James Clarke, 1994), p 180.
[8] The Edwardian Injunctions 1547, O4, in Bray (ed) *Documents*, p 249.

and finished with the section on The Lord's Prayer, thereby lacking any material on the sacraments. The reason why this version lacked sacramental teaching is not known, but it may have been because the bishops were not in agreement about the theology of the Lord's Supper or because discussion of the Lord's Supper would be likely to stir up dissension among the people. It may also have been felt that the Prayer Book orders of service provided a sufficient guide to the meaning of the sacraments.

The 1549 version was re-issued with some slight alterations in wording in the *Second Prayer Book* of 1552. The 1552 Prayer Book was abolished during the reign of Queen Mary and the use of the Catechism was abolished with it. In his imprisonment under Queen Mary, Nicholas Ridley lamented that:

> ...the Catechism which was lately set forth in the English tongue, was now in every pulpit condemned. Satan could not endure that so much light should be spread abroad; for he knew that nothing tended so effectually to overturn his kingdom, as for children to learn Christ from their infancy; by which means not only children, but those of riper years also would, together with the children, necessarily learn Christ.[9]

However, plans for a new Catechism giving expression to Roman Catholic theology came to nothing because of the death of Queen Mary in 1558 and the subsequent return by Queen Elizabeth I to the religious policies of her father and brother.

This return led to the issuing in 1559 of a slightly revised form of the *Second Prayer Book*. In this revision the Confirmation service, and with it the Catechism, remained unchanged. Queen Elizabeth's injunctions to the Church in 1559 laid down that:

> ...every parson, vicar and curate shall upon every holy day and every second Sunday in the year, hear and instruct all the youth of the parish for half an hour in the least, before Evening Prayer, in the Ten Commandments, the Articles of the Belief, and the Lord's Prayer, and diligently examine them, and teach the Catechism set forth in the book of public prayer.[10]

---

[9] Quoted in E B Redlitch, *The Church Catechism*, (London: Macmillan, 1924), p 90.
[10] The Elizabethan Injunctions 1559, 44, in Bray (ed) *Documents*, p 344.

During the reign of Queen Elizabeth three other catechisms in Latin and English by the Dean of St Paul's, Alexander Nowell, (the *Large, Middle* and *Little Catechisms*) were authorised by the Church of England. The Catechism in the Prayer Book remained the authorised manual of basic religious instruction for all young people, but it was now supplemented by the other three catechisms which were more detailed and contained material on the sacraments. The idea was that together they would provide the basis for an educational curriculum that would give young people a course of religious instruction and also help to teach them both English and Latin.

The *Constitutions and Canons Ecclesiastical* of 1571 reiterated the requirement for the Prayer Book Catechism to be taught by the clergy to all young people and reminded the laity that they needed to learn the Catechism as a preliminary to admission to Holy Communion, marriage and acting as a Godparent at baptism.

It was a complaint of the Puritan party in the Church of England that the Prayer Book Catechism was too short. However, at the Hampton Court Conference of 1604 at the beginning of the reign of James I the Puritan representatives agreed to accept the continued use of the existing Catechism providing something were added 'for the doctrine of the sacrament.' The Dean of St Paul's, John Overall, was instructed to make this addition and a few changes of wording to the existing sections were made at the same time.

The Canons of 1604 also laid down that that the clergy were to 'catechise every Sunday.' Canon LIX stated:

> Every Parson, Vicar or Curate, upon every Sunday and Holy-day before Evening Prayer, shall for half an hour or more, examine and instruct the Youth, and ignorant Persons of his Parish, in the Ten Commandments, the Articles of the Belief, and in the Lord's Prayer: and shall diligently hear, instruct, and teach them the Catechism set forth in the Book of Common Prayer. And all Fathers, Mothers, Masters and Mistresses, shall cause their Children, Servants and Apprentices, which have not learned the Catechism, to come to the Church at the time appointed, obediently to hear, and to be ordered by the Minister, until they have learned the same. And if any Minister neglect his Duty herein, let him be sharply reproved upon the first Complaint, and true Notice thereof given to the Bishop or Ordinary of the Place. If after submitting himself, he shall wifully offend therein again, let him be suspended. If so the third time, there being little hope that he will be therein reformed, then

excommunicated, and so remain until he will be reformed. And likewise, if any of the said Fathers, Mothers, Masters or Mistresses, Children, Servants, or Apprentices shall neglect their Duties, as the one sort in not causing them to come, and the other in refusing to learn as aforesaid; let them be suspended by their Ordinaries, (if they be not Children) and if they so persist by the space of a Month, then let them be Excommunicated.

The 1604 Catechism, together with the rest of the Prayer Book, was abolished by Parliament during the Commonwealth and replaced by the *Westminster Shorter Catechism,* However, following the Restoration of the monarchy in 1660, it was re-issued with the rest of the *Book of Common Prayer* in 1662. It was printed separately from the Confirmation service and a range of additional amendments were made to the 1604 text which gave us the Catechism we still have today.

Nowell's catechisms dropped out of use and the 1662 Catechism remained the sole authorised Church of England catechism until the *Revised Catechism* was issued in 1962.

The base text of the Catechism is the 1549 text with a few stylistic revisions, intended to make the Catechism more grammatical or more accurate in expression. None of them was intended to change its theology. The section on the sacraments which was added in 1604 was probably taken from the writings of the author of the rest of the Catechism, thus ensuring theological coherence between this new section and what precedes it. In summary, although the Catechism developed to some extent between 1549 and 1662, the end product reflects the same coherent theological vision that animated the original text.

2.2 The Authorship of the Catechism

Like the rest of the *Book of Common Prayer,* the Catechism is anonymous. However, we know that the section on the sacraments was the work of John Overall who produced it by abridging existing material on the sacraments in the *Middle* and *Little Catechisms* of Alexander Nowell. There is also both external and internal evidence that Nowell was the author of the original 1549 version.

The external evidence is Izaak Walton's *The Complete Angler* and Ralph Churton's *Life of Alexander Nowell,* both of which attribute the Catechism to Nowell on the basis of evidence now lost to us. The internal evidence is the verbatim agreement between the 1549 Catechism and the corresponding sections of Nowell's *Little Catechism* (which also seems to have been originally written in the reign of Edward VI). To quote Redlich, 'Nowell, if he wrote the Little Catechism, must have written the Catechism of 1549.'[11]

However, if Nowell did write the Catechism, he did not write it in isolation. His work will have been revised and reviewed by those responsible for the *First Prayer Book* as a whole and they may have been responsible for suggesting some of its content. It has been suggested, for instance, that Thomas Cranmer may have been responsible for the distinctive introduction to the Lord's Prayer which is not a question but a brief exposition of the need for grace to obey the commandments, and that Hugh Latimer may have been responsible for the words 'state of salvation' in the opening section.

Furthermore, we know that Nowell did not start from scratch in writing the Catechism. Instead he built on an existing document, *The Necessary Doctrine and Erudition for Any Christian Man*, popularly known as the King's Book, which had been published in 1543 by royal authority and with the approval of Parliament and the Convocation of Canterbury. In the words of Redlich, a comparison of the Catechism with the *Necessary Doctrine* shows that 'its phraseology is to be primarily traced to it; the order in which the Creed, the Ten Commandments and Lord's Prayer are placed, the versions of these fundamentals of our faith, and many a little detail are due to its influence.'[12]

In 1549 *The Necessary Doctrine* was the Church of England's authorised statement of faith. It was a statement that reflected the move back to a more conservative Catholicism that took place at the end of the reign of Henry VIII. It emphasised traditional Catholic theology by teaching the legitimacy of receiving communion in one kind, the necessity of priestly absolution as part of the sacrament of penance, and the importance of the performance of good works for the 'increase of justification'. It reiterated the requirement of celibacy for the clergy and those who had taken monastic vows, and over against the Protestant belief that everyone should be able to read the Bible, it restricted the reading of the Scripture to the clergy and those of gentle birth.

---

[11] Redlitch, *The Church Catechism*, p 146. For a more detailed examination of the evidence concerning authorship see Redlich chapters VI and VII.
[12] Redlitch, *The Church Catechism*, p 67.

None of this is reflected in the Catechism. Nowell took what he wanted from this authorised statement and used it to create a new theological statement that was in line with the Protestant convictions that were shared by Nowell and other leaders of the Church of England during the reign of Edward VI.

3 The Structure of the Catechism

The Catechism falls into five clear sections. The first section (the first four questions and answers) set out in general terms the obligation of the baptised Christian to live out the baptismal covenant. The remaining four sections then explain what this means in more detail.

In his commentary on the Catechism, Frank Colquhoun helpfully sets out this fivefold structure as follows:

I. *The Christian Covenant*, of which baptism is the visible sign and seal. There are two sides to this covenant. On his part, God promises us a place in the Church, his family and kingdom; on our part, we pledge ourselves to renounce evil, to believe the truth, and to do what is right.

II. *The Apostles' Creed* comes next, as setting forth the content of the Christian faith to which the baptismal covenant binds us.

III. *The Ten Commandments* make clear what is meant by doing what is right and how this works in practice, viz. in duty to God and to our neighbour.

IV. *The Lord's Prayer* illustrates and expands the reference to prayer in the answer to the fourth question: 'I pray unto God to give me his grace...'

V. *The Sacraments* show us how this grace of God is donated to us through Christ's own appointed ordinances: initially in baptism, whereby we are admitted into the Christian covenant: and subsequently in the Lord's Supper, whereby our covenant union with the Lord is constantly renewed.[1]

Theologically, this structure tells us that our actions done in obedience to the law of God are surrounded by the grace of God. In the opening section it is God's grace given to us in baptism that is basis for our obedience and it is God's grace given to us in answer to prayer that makes obedience possible. In the remaining four sections it is the gracious action of God summarised in the Creed in section two that precedes, and is the context for, the Commandments in section three. It

---

[1] F Colquhoun, *The Catechism and the Order of Confirmation*, (London: Hodder and Stoughton, 1963), p 15.

is as the people created, redeemed and sanctified by God that we are called to obey the Commandments. Sections four and five then tell us how the grace of God is given to us in answer to prayer and through the sacraments so that we can obey the Commandments.

This commentary on the Catechism will follow the fivefold structure set out by Colquhoun, looking at each section in turn.

4 The Teaching of the Catechism

4.1 *The Christian Covenant*

The opening section of the Catechism begins by looking back to the giving of a name in the Baptism service. In the services for the Baptism of infants in the *Book of Common Prayer* the Priest baptises the child in the name given by the Godparents. That is what is being referred to in the opening two questions and answers here. The Catechism starts by enquiring about the name given at Baptism because of the way in which name and identity go together. Someone's name marks them off as a particular individual with a particular identity.

It goes on to ask who gave them this name in order to highlight the fact that the fundamental identity of the person who has been baptised is that given to them by God in Baptism. Somebody's surname declares that they were born of two earthly parents. It identifies them as member of a specific human family. Their baptismal name, by contrast, declares that through their Baptism they were born 'not of blood, nor of the will of the flesh nor of the will of man, but of God' (John 1:13) and are therefore members of God's family, the Church.

Because this new identity is given at Baptism the Catechism then says 'wherein I was made a member of Christ, the child of God, and an inheritor of the kingdom of heaven.' 'Wherein' means 'at this point' and what the Catechism is saying is that when they received their new identity at Baptism they became what they were not before, namely a member of the body of Christ (1 Corinthians 12:12-13), a child of God who can call God 'Abba, Father' (Galatians 3:27-4:6), and someone who has inherited a place in God's kingdom (Titus 3:4-7, 1 Peter 1:3-4). In the words of Bishop Thomas Ken, it follows that 'the happiness of a good Christian is altogether unutterable; he is one who has Christ for his head, God for his Father, and heaven, with all its joys and glories, which are eternal, for his inheritance.'[1]

These opening questions and answers highlight the divine side of the Christian Covenant. They emphasise the way in which God has given a new identity to someone who has been baptised as a pure

---

[1] Ken, *Practice of Divine Love*, p 2.

gratuitous gift which they have done nothing to earn or deserve. The next two questions and answers then turn to look at the human side of the Covenant; what the person who has been baptised needs to do in response to the gift they have been given.

As before, this second set of questions and answers looks back to the Baptism service, in which the Priest asks the Godparents three questions which they answer in the name of the child. Do they renounce the devil and all his works, the vain pomp and glory of the world and the carnal desires of the flesh? Do they believe in the faith set out in the Apostles Creed? Will they obey God's will and commandments? It is these questions, answered in the affirmative by the Godparents, which are recalled here.

Specifically, the Catechism says that in response to the questions asked by the priest the Godparents promised that the child being baptised would renounce three things:

(1) 'The devil and all his works.' This means both the devil himself and the sinful thoughts and actions which he inspires (1 Peter 5:8-9, 1 John 3:8).

(2) 'The pomps and vanity of this wicked world.' This means all the things in this world which lead us away from God (1 John 2:15-17). They are called 'pomps' and vanities,' things that are an empty show, in order to make the point that while they may superficially appear glamorous and attractive they are in reality ephemeral in comparison with the 'solid joys and lasting treasures' of the kingdom of God.

(3) 'The sinful lusts of the flesh.' This means the sins arising from the desires of our fallen human nature (Galatians 5:16-24).

It further says that the Godparents promised that the child would believe 'the articles of the Christian faith,' the fundamentals of the Christian faith set out in the Apostles Creed.

Finally it says that they promised that the child would obey 'God's will and commandments.' This means everything that God wants us to do and, in particular, the summary of this given to us in the Ten Commandments in Exodus 20:2-17 and Deuteronomy 5:6-21.

In the words of Colquhoun, the existence of these promises makes the point that:

There is nothing magical about baptism. As a sacrament of the gospel, it offers something to us, for it is of the nature of the gospel to *give*. But equally as a sacrament of the gospel it asks something from us, for it is also the nature of the gospel to require an answer, to make a demand.[2]

As W H Griffith Thomas points out, these promises:

> ...express our entire responsibility to God, and for the longest and most varied life these three sum up everything that man can be or do in relation to God. They express our attitude to sin in repentance and our attitude to God in trust and obedience, and they are thus absolutely essential to all Christian living. It is impossible to conceive of our receiving God's gifts unless we are in the right attitude towards God suggested by these requirements. No realization and enjoyment of the blessing of being 'a member of Christ' is possible apart from repentance, nor can I fully understand what it means to 'the child of God' apart from trust in my heavenly Father, while my position as 'an inheritor of the kingdom of heaven' is quite impossible unless I am obedient to our Heavenly King. Thus our responsibilities correspond to God's gifts, and are the natural and necessary answer of the soul to the offer of God's mercy and grace in Christ.[3]

It is because this is the case that in the last question and answer in this section of the Catechism the answer to the question 'Dost thou not think that thou art bound to believe, and to do, as they have promised for thee?' is 'Yes verily: and by God's help so I will.' The point here is not that the person who has been baptised is bound by the mere fact of promises having been made on their behalf – if, for example, what was promised was something wrong then a promise ought not to be kept. The point is rather that these promises ought to be kept because they express the duty that we owe to God because of what he has done for us. To quote Griffith Thomas again:

> Duty means that which is 'due' to God from us, and God's 'due' is our whole-hearted allegiance, loyalty and obedience. Conscience whispers 'I ought' and 'I ought' means 'I owe it.' I owe it to my God and Father to give Him my life's trust and love and our Church puts this answer into our mouths as the natural, right, and only possible

---

[2] Colquhoun, *Catechism and Confirmation*, p 15.
[3] W H Griffith Thomas, *The Catholic Faith*, (London: Church Book Room Press, 1960), p 11.

response to God.[4]

The answer goes on to say 'I heartily thank our heavenly Father, that he hath called me to this state of salvation, through Jesus Christ our Saviour.' The significance of these words is that they make clear that the state of salvation to which God has called us through baptism is one that involves repentance, trust and obedience. It is a state in which we actively respond to what God has done for us.

However, this does not mean that being saved is dependent on our own efforts, as if God did his bit at our baptism and we now have to do ours. We remain dependent on God's grace for our salvation. This is why the final sentence of the answer declares 'And I pray to God to give me his grace that I may continue in the same unto my life's end.' The Anglican Reformers of the sixteenth century believed (in line with New Testament passages such as Matthew 10:22, Luke 8:13, John 15:5-6, Hebrews 10:39) that it was possible for people who had been called by God to salvation to fall away from Him[5] and they also believed that the remedy against this was both strenuous effort on the behalf of the believer and a constant seeking for God's grace which alone made such effort possible. They believed with St Paul that it was only because 'God is at work in you, to will and to work for his good pleasure' that it is possible for believers 'to work out your own salvation with fear and trembling' (Philippians 2:12-13) and they therefore believed that it was continually necessary to ask God in prayer to be at work in this way.

4.2   The Apostles Creed

At the Reformation the Church of England retained the three Creeds that were in use in the Western Church during the Middle Ages: the Apostles Creed, the Nicene Creed and the Athanasian Creed. As Article VIII of the Thirty Nine Articles explains, the English Reformers believed that these Creeds 'ought thoroughly to be received and believed: for they may be proved by the most certain warrants of Holy Scripture.'

The Apostles Creed had its origins in the profession of faith made by candidates at their Baptism, and during the Middle Ages it was the Creed that was used in the Baptism service in the Western Church. In

---

[4] Griffith Thomas, *The Catholic Faith*, p 11.
[5] The homily 'How dangerous it is to fall away from God' in the *First Book of Homilies* addresses this issue in detail.

line with this traditional Western practice the *Book of Common Prayer* uses an interrogative form of the Apostles Creed as the profession of faith made by Godparents on behalf of those being baptised. By reciting it they are re-affirming the profession of faith made on their behalf at their Baptism.

If we turn to the threefold answer given in the Catechism to the question 'What dost thou chiefly learn in these Articles of thy Belief?' we find that that the answer affirms both the identity and activity of God. It talks about who God is and what God does.

In terms of who God is, the Catechism affirms belief in God the Father, God the Son and God the Holy Ghost (Ghost being the sixteenth century English word for Spirit). The English Reformers, in line with the teaching of the Church from the earliest times, did not see this as involving belief in three separate Gods, but in one God who exists as three persons at one and the same time. In the words of the Athanasian Creed 'the Father is God, the Son is God and the Holy Ghost is God. And yet there are not three Gods: but one God.'

The biblical basis for this belief is helpfully summarised by Griffith Thomas, who argues that in the New Testament we find two lines of teaching:

(a) One line of teaching insists on the unity of the Godhead (1 Corinthians 8:4; James 2:19); and

(b) the other reveals distinctions within the Godhead (Matthew 3:16, 17; 28:19, 2 Corinthians 13:14).

We see clearly that

(1) the Father is God (Matthew 11:25; Romans 15:6; Ephesians 4:6);

(2) the Son is God John 1:1, 18; 20:28; Acts 20:28; Romans 9:5; Hebrews 1:8; Colossians 2:9; Philippians 2:6; 2 Peter 1:1);

(3) the Holy Spirit is God (Acts 5:3, 4; 1 Corinthians 2:10, 11; Ephesians 2:22);

(4) the Father, Son and Holy Spirit are distinct from one another, sending and being sent, honouring and being honoured. The Father honours the Son, the Son honours the Father, and the Holy Spirit honours the Son (John 15:26; 16:13,14; 17:1,8, 18, 23).

(5) Nevertheless, whatever relations of subordination there may be between the Persons in the working out of redemption, the

Three are alike regarded as God. The doctrine of the Trinity is the correlation, embodiment and synthesis of the teaching of these passages.[6]

In terms of what God does, the Catechism affirms that as Father, Son and Holy Ghost, God creates (Malachi 2:10, 1 Corinthians 8:6), redeems (Luke 1:68, Galatians 3:13) and sanctifies (2 Thessalonians 2:13, 1 Peter 1:2). The Catechism itself does not explain what it means to believe that God creates, redeems and sanctifies us. However, a classic explanation dating from the time of Reformation and in line with the theology of the English Reformers is provided by Martin Luther in his *Small Catechism*.

Luther declares that faith in God the Father as creator means:

> I believe that God has created me and all that exists; that he has given me and still sustains my body and soul, all my limbs and senses, my reason and all the faculties of my mind, together with food and clothing, house and home, family and property; that he provides me daily and abundantly with all the necessities of life, protects me from all danger and preserves me from all evil. All this he does out of his pure, fatherly, and divine goodness and mercy, without any merit or worthiness on my part. For all of this I am bound to thank, praise, serve and obey him. This is most certainly true.[7]

Faith in God the Son as redeemer means:

> I believe that Jesus Christ, true God, begotten of the Father from all eternity, and also true man, born of the virgin Mary, is my Lord, who has redeemed me, a lost and condemned creature, delivered me and freed me from all sins, from death, and from the power of the devil, not with silver and gold but with his holy and precious blood and with his innocent sufferings and death, in order that I may be his, live under him in his kingdom, and serve him in everlasting righteousness, innocence, and blessedness, even as he is risen from the dead and lives and reigns to all eternity. This is most

---

[6] W H Griffith Thomas *The Principles of Theology*, (London: Church Book Room Press 1951), p. 24. For a detailed exploration of these passages see A W Wainwright, *The Trinity in the New Testament*, (London: SPCK, 1962) and E J Fortman, *The Triune God*, (London: Hutchinson, 1972).

[7] M Luther *Small Catechism*, in M A Knoll (ed), *Confessions and Catechisms of the Reformation*, (Vancouver: Regent College Publishing, 1991), p 68.

certainly true.[8]

Faith in God the Holy Spirit as sanctifier means:

> I believe that by my own reason or strength I cannot believe in Jesus Christ, my Lord, or come to him. But the Holy Spirit has called me through the gospel, enlightened me with his gifts, and sanctified and preserved me in true faith, just as he calls, gathers, enlightens and sanctifies the whole Christian church on earth and preserves it in union with Jesus Christ in the one true faith. In this Christian church he daily and abundantly forgives all my sins, and the sins of all believers, and on the last day he will raise me and all the dead and will grant eternal life to me and all who believe in Christ, this is most certainly true.[9]

As Arthur Robinson notes in his *Church Catechism Explained*, the threefold summary of the Creed given in the Catechism describes 'three gradually lessening circles':

> 'First, I learn to believe in God the Father, who hath made me, and *all the world.*' That is the Circle of Creation, wide enough to embrace the whole round world and all that therein is. 'Secondly, in God the Son, who hath redeemed me, and *all mankind.*' That is the Circle of Redemption, not so large as the first but yet large enough to include all the men, women and children who ever have lived, or ever shall live: the whole race, the entire kind of man. 'Thirdly in God the Holy Ghost, who sanctifieth me, and *all the elect people of God.*' This is the innermost circle of all, the Circle of Election; a much smaller one, containing only a portion of mankind, gathered out from the rest to be members of the Society of which the Creed itself speaks as the Church.[10]

The idea that there is an inner circle of the elect distinguished from the rest of humankind is a stumbling block for many people. The problem they have with this idea is that, to quote Oliver O'Donovan, it seems to imply 'a self-justifying division of mankind into two camps; this division serves no purpose in redemption but is simply given.'[11] Put another way, it seems to suggest that God engages in arbitrary favouritism.

---

[8] Knoll (ed), *Confessions*, pp 68-69.
[9] Knoll (ed), *Confessions*, p 69.
[10] A Robinson, *The Church Catechism Explained*, (Cambridge: CUP, 1903), p 44.
[11] O O'Donovan, *On the Thirty Nine Articles*, (Exeter: Paternoster Press, 1986), p 83.

However, when we look at the doctrine of election in biblical terms we see that God's choice of some people is not an arbitrary decision that they should enjoy a salvation that is denied to others. Rather, God chooses people precisely so that those who are chosen may be the vehicles through which His salvation can be shared with those around them.

Understood in this way, election is not a contradiction of the truth that 'God desires all men to be saved and come to a knowledge of the truth' (1 Timothy 2:4). It is, rather, the means by which this truth is put into effect as God works out His purposes in human history. As Karl Barth insists, we cannot 'make the open number of those who are elect in Jesus Christ into a closed number to which all other men are opposed as if they were rejected.'[12] We have instead to think in terms of God's eternal will to bless humankind in Christ being put into effect in history through his constant calling of individual men and women both to enjoy this blessing for themselves and to be the means which God uses to call others so that they can enjoy it too.

4.3 The Ten Commandments

In the Old Testament the Ten Commandments given by God to Moses on Mount Sinai at the time of the Exodus and recorded in Exodus 20:2-17 and Deuteronomy 5:6-21 are seen as the basic form of God's law to His people which the other biblical laws then expand. In the New Testament likewise the Ten Commandments are seen as the basic commandments which God's people are expected to observe (see for example Matthew 19:16-22 and Romans 13:8-10).

The Catechism follows this biblical pattern by setting out the Ten Commandments as the commandments which those who have been baptised need to obey.

It first of all gives the text of the Ten Commandments, using the version contained in *A Necessary Doctrine and Erudition for any Christian Man*. It then gives a summary of what it thinks a Christian should learn from a study of the Commandments ('What dost thou chiefly learn from these Commandments?'). Following Jesus' twofold summary of the law in terms of love of God and love of neighbour (Matthew 22:37-39) the

---

[12] K Barth, *Church Dogmatics* II.2 (Edinburgh: T&T Clark 1957), p 422.

Catechism divides the commandments into 'my duty towards God' (Commandments 1-4) and 'my duty towards my Neighbour' (Commandments 6-10). Under each of these two headings it then gives 'a simple practical explanation of the commandments with a view to making clear how they are intended to work out in the life of a Christian.'[13] For reasons which remain unclear the explanation of the seventh commandment ('thou shalt not commit adultery') was placed after the explanation of the ninth commandment ('thou shalt not bear false witness). Because it expounds the duty that the Christian owes God, this section of the Catechism is often referred to as 'the Duty.'

The Catechism's account of 'my duty towards God' begins with a general statement of the Christian's duty towards God: 'My duty towards God is to believe in him, to fear him, and to love him, with all my heart, with all my mind, with all my soul, and with all my strength.' The duty to believe in God and to fear him is derived from biblical passages such as Hebrews 11:6 and Proverbs 19:23 and the duty to love God is taken from Jesus' teaching in Mark 12:29-30.

It then goes on to explain what it means to obey the first four Commandments.

Obedience to the first two Commandments 'Thou shalt have none other gods but me' and 'Thou shalt not make to thyself any graven image, nor the likeness of any thing that is in heaven above, or in the earth beneath, or in the water under the earth. Thou shalt not bow down to them, nor worship them' is explained in terms of the duty to worship God and 'to give him thanks, to put my whole trust in him, to call upon him.' What the Catechism does is to convert the biblical prohibitions into positive statements of what the Christian should do based on biblical texts such as Psalm 95:6, Psalm 105:1 and Isaiah 26:4, on the grounds that someone who is truly worshipping, thanking, trusting and calling upon God will not be worshiping other gods or creating idols.

In similar fashion the prohibition in the third commandment 'Thou shalt not take the Name of the Lord thy God in vain' is converted into the positive duty 'to honour his holy Name and his Word.' The reason for the inclusion of God's 'Word' here is that it is impossible to honour who God is (God's Name) without also honouring God's written self-revelation contained in Scripture (God's Word). The two necessarily go together.

---

[13] Colquhoun, *Catechism and Confirmation*. p 93.

Finally, the Catechism expands the Command to 'keep holy the Sabbath day' into a duty to serve God truly 'all the days of my life.' In 1661 the Puritans sought to persuade the bishops to expand this duty by adding the words 'particularly on the Lord's day.' As Robinson notes, 'the Bishops declined, being satisfied no doubt that the words as they stood sufficiently enforced the duty of a proper observance of Sunday, while they also pointed to the consecration of all time as the great end for the attainment of which the Sabbath was originally instituted.'[14] As he further notes, the fourth Commandment, 'by requiring six days of labour as well as one day of rest, does actually enjoin a service which is to include '*all* the days' of our life.[15]

The Catechism's account of 'My duty towards my Neighbour' once again begins with a general statement of the Christian's duty in this regard ('to love him as myself, and to do to all men as I would they should do unto me', taken from Jesus' teaching in Mark 12:31 and Matthew 7:12). It then gives an explanation of each Commandment in turn, in each case giving a duty based on the fundamental ethical principle underlying the specific command.

The fifth commandment 'Honour thy father and thy mother' is expanded into a wider duty to not only 'love, honour, and succour my father and mother' but also 'honour and obey the Queen, and all that are put in authority under her: To submit myself to all my governors, teachers, spiritual pastors and masters: To order myself lowly and reverently to all my betters.' The basic principle here is seen as the duty to give due respect to those in authority ('respect to whom respect is due, honour to whom honour is due' Romans 13:7) with the duty to honour parents being the basic, but not the exclusive, example of this. In the words of Archbishop Wake, the Catechism holds that Commandment 'expressly regards only our natural parents; but the reason of it extends to all sorts of persons who are in any respect our superiors and to whom we owe any singular honour on that account.'[16]

The sixth commandment 'Thou shalt do no murder' is seen as expressing the principle that we should refrain from any action that will harm our neighbour or any desire to cause such harm. The duty

---

[14] Robinson, *The Church Catechism Explained*, p 85.
[15] Robinson, *The Church Catechism Explained*, p 85.
[16] William Wake, *The Principles of the Christian Religion Explained*, (London: T Cadell, 1827), p 230.

therefore becomes 'To hurt nobody by word nor deed…To bear no malice nor hatred in my heart.' In including not only actual harm, but also the desire to cause harm, the Catechism is echoing biblical passages such as Matthew 5:21-22 and 1 John 3:15.

The seventh commandment 'Thou shalt not commit adultery' is seen as expressing the principle that we should keep our bodies under proper control. Hence the corresponding duty is 'To keep my body in temperance, soberness, and chastity.' The terms used here are general rather than specific, involving not only restraint in regard to alcohol and sex (which is what the terms suggest in modern parlance) but a general pattern of purity and self-restraint as advocated in New Testament passages such as Romans 13:13-14 and Colossians 3:5-8. To quote Wake again, we are 'to be modest in our behaviour: grave and chaste in our conversation: to regulate, as much as may be, our very thoughts and desires.'[17]

The eighth commandment 'thou shalt not steal' is seen to involve what Wake calls 'all kind of unlawful getting or detaining of any thing whereby another is injured, or oppressed, in what of right belongs, or ought to belong' to him.'[18] The duty corresponding to this is seen as twofold; positively, 'To be true and just in all my dealing' and negatively, 'To keep my hands from picking and stealing.' 'Picking' means 'pilfering or petty stealing'[19] and the purpose of pairing this with 'stealing' is to make the point that we are to refrain from all theft, however insignificant or trivial it may appear. The biblical basis for this comprehensive view of the Commandment can be found in Leviticus 19:11-13 'You shall not steal, nor deal falsely, nor lie to one another… You shall not oppress your neighbour or rob him. The wages of a hired servant shall not remain with you all night unto the morning.'[20]

---

[17] Wake, *Principles*, p 261.
[18] Wake, *Principles*, p 264.
[19] Robinson, *The Church Catechism Explained*, p 93.
[20] As Gordon Wenham notes in his commentary on Leviticus the point of the prohibition in v13 against keeping the wages of a hired servant overnight is that a day labourer could expect to be paid in the evening (Matthew 20:8) and 'to delay payment till the following morning might not be illegal, but it could cause great hardship to a poor man and his family' (G Wenham, *The Book of Leviticus*, Grand Rapids, Eerdmans 1979), p 268.

The ninth commandment 'Thou shalt not bear false witness against thy neighbour' is understood to prohibit not only telling lies against someone in court, but more widely saying anything evil or malicious against other people. The Christian's duty is therefore '[To keep] my tongue from evil-speaking, lying, and slandering.' This duty of keeping a guard on our tongue echoes biblical passages such as Psalm 15:3, Matthew 12:36-37 and Ephesians 4:25 and 29.

The tenth commandment, 'Thou shalt not covet thy neighbour's house, thou shalt not covet thy neighbour's wife, nor his servant, nor his maid, nor his ox, nor his ass, nor any thing that is his' is understood to involve not only not coveting our neighbour's possessions, but a willingness to accept and work diligently in that state of life in which God places us at any given time. It follows that the duty is 'Not to covet nor desire other men's goods; but to learn and labour truly to get mine own living, and to do my duty in that state of life, unto which it shall please God to call me.' The biblical basis for this duty is biblical passages such as Luke 12:15, 1 Corinthians 7:17-24 and 1 Thessalonians 4:11-12. As Robinson explains, this duty does not mean:

> ...that a child is of necessity to remain in the social position to which he was born. The words of the Catechism are constantly misquoted as if they were 'unto which it *hath pleased*,' instead of 'unto which it *shall please* God to call me.' For anything he knows to the contrary, the child may yet be called to fill a very different position from that in which he began.[21]

As he goes on to say:

> What is forbidden is that eager restless longing, or empty idle wishing, for a change of circumstance, which quickly breeds ill-will towards others and wastes time and strength in useless dreams and selfish repinings. It is this temper which is fatal towards any right discharge of present duty.[22]

4.4 The Lord's Prayer

At this point the Catechism returns to the need to pray to God for grace which was first mentioned in the fourth answer in the opening section.

---

[21] Wenham, *The Book of Leviticus*, p 95.
[22] Wenham, *The Book of Leviticus*, p 96.

In this section the need to pray for grace is linked to what has previously been said about the duty of the Christian to obey the Ten Commandments. The Catechist informs the child being catechised that they cannot obey the Commandments without God's 'special grace', which the child needs to learn to call for at all times by 'diligent prayer.' By God's 'special grace' the Catechism means the grace which God gives to his people to redeem, sanctify and glorify them (Romans 8:28-30). It is called 'special grace' in distinction from the 'common grace' by which God maintains all people in existence, limits the effects of sin through the existence of conscience and of civil government, and permits human beings to make advances in fields such as technology and medicine. By 'diligent prayer' the Catechism means the kind of serious persistent calling upon God taught by Jesus in Matthew 7:7-11 and Luke 11:5-13.

The Catechist then asks the child if they can recite the Lord's Prayer on the grounds that this is the model prayer given to us by Jesus himself (Matthew 6:7-15, Luke 11: 1-4), which includes in summary form everything that the Christian ever needs to ask for from God. If the child is able to recite this prayer and mean it, then they know how to pray.

After this introduction the Catechism goes on to give the text of the Lord's Prayer, using a version that is almost identical with that used in the *Necessary Doctrine* of 1543, which omits the doxology found in some texts of Matthew 6:13. The text is followed by an exposition of the meaning of the Lord's Prayer, often known as 'the Desire' because it sets out what the child being catechised desires from God.

The exposition begins by describing the God to whom the Lord's Prayer is addressed, glossing 'Our Father who art in heaven' as 'my Lord God our heavenly Father, who is the giver of all goodness.' As Colquhoun comments, these words put us in mind of God's:

> ...sovereign power and authority; his fatherly love and care for his children; and his lavish generosity in meeting their needs. With this conception clearly before us we shall know how to draw near to him: with reverence, with confidence and with gratitude.[23]

The Catechism then adds that I desire this God 'to send His grace unto me, and to all people.' These words have no direct basis in the text of the Lord's Prayer itself, but they are added to make it clear that what is

---

[23] Colquhoun, *Catechism and Confirmation*, p 124.

asked for in the Lord' Prayer is the grace that is needed to enable us to fulfil our baptismal vows by living in accordance with God's commandments. That is to say, the petitions in the Lord's Prayer tell us what grace actually means.

The reason that the Catechism asks that God will send his grace not only to me but 'to all people' was that the English Reformers believed that we should not exclude anyone from the scope of the word 'us' in the Lord's Prayer. What we ask for in the Lord's Prayer we ask for not only for ourselves, but for everyone else as well on the grounds that in the same way that the promises of God in Holy Scripture are to be understood 'generally' (Article XVII), that is to say as potentially applicable to everyone, so every human being is to be seen as a potential recipient of the grace asked for in the Lord's Prayer. This being the case, charity requires that we pray for all human beings. In the words of Bishop Ken:

> Glory be to thee, O Lord, who in teaching me to call God Our Father, hath taught me not to confine my charity to myself, but to pray also with the affections of a Brother, and to inlarge it (Ephesians 4:6, 1 Peter 3:18) to all Mankind, who are children by creation; to all Christians, who are Children by adoption, of the same heavenly Father. O give me that brotherly kindness to them all, that I may beg the same blessings for them as for myself, and earnestly pray, that they may all share with me in thy fatherly love.[24]

The Catechism next expounds 'Hallowed be thy Name, Thy kingdom come, Thy will be done, in earth as it is in heaven' as meaning 'that we may worship him, serve him, and obey him, as we ought to do.' The reason the Catechism expounds this section of the Lord's Prayer in this way is to make the point that what the coming of God's kingdom and the doing of God's will means is a state of affairs in which human beings worship, serve and obey God. That is what they are meant to do and that is what we pray for.

'Give us this day our daily bread' is expounded as meaning 'I pray unto God, that he will send us all things that be needful both for our souls and bodies.' 'Daily bread' is understood as meaning that which we need as human beings day by day and since we are not only bodies with physical needs but also souls with spiritual needs this petition is seen as

---

[24] Ken, *Practice of Divine Love*, p 98.

covering both. This interpretation is in line with the teaching of some of the early Fathers who saw in the word 'bread' a reference not only to earthly food but to the 'bread of life' given to us by Jesus (John 6:35-51).

'And forgive us our trespasses, As we forgive them that trespass against us' is understood as meaning 'that he will be merciful unto us, and forgive us our sins.' At first sight it seems odd that the Catechism makes no reference to our forgiving others. However, the explanation is probably that the Catechism wants us to view the whole of the Lord's Prayer in terms of what we ask for from God.

This means that the fourth petition of the Lord's Prayer should not be seen as meaning that we ask God to forgive us because we have forgiven other people. Rather, we ask God to make us people who sins can be forgiven because we forgive others. See in this light both parts of the fourth petition are included in the desire that God will be merciful to us. Everything depends upon God's mercy because 'forgiveness is nor a prize which we win by our own merits but a gift which we receive as result of God's free bounty.'[25]

The final petition 'And lead us not into temptation, But deliver us from evil' is interpreted in terms of a desire that it will please God 'to save and defend us in all dangers ghostly and bodily; and that he will keep us from all sin and wickedness, and from our ghostly enemy, and from everlasting death.' There is a long standing debate about whether 'evil' in this part of the Lord's Prayer means 'evil' or 'the evil one' (the original Greek could be translated either way) and the interpretation in the Catechism supports both. It asks for a comprehensive deliverance from all forms of evil both temporal and spiritual ('ghostly') and from the devil ('our ghostly enemy'). Everlasting death (the 'second death' referred to Revelation 20:14) is mentioned as the final and most serious evil from which we seek to be delivered.

The Catechism finishes its exposition of the Lord's Prayer by explaining that the Hebrew word 'Amen' should be understood to mean 'So be it' and that the reason that we say 'so be it' is because we trust that in his mercy and goodness God the Father will grant what we ask for 'through our Lord Jesus Christ.'

The best way of understanding the significance of 'through our Lord Jesus Christ' is with reference to the words of St. Paul in Romans 8:31-39:

---

[25] Colquhoun, *Catechism and Confirmation*, p 128.

What then shall we say to this? If God is for us, who is against us? He who did not spare his own Son but gave him up for us all, will he not also give us all things with him? Who shall bring any charge against God's elect? It is God who justifies; who is to condemn? Is it Christ Jesus, who died, yes, who was raised from the dead, who is at the right hand of God, who indeed intercedes for us? Who shall separate us from the love of Christ? Shall tribulation, or distress, or persecution, or famine, or nakedness, or peril, or sword? As it is written 'For thy sake we are being killed all the day long; we are regarded as sheep to be slaughtered.' No, in all these things we are more than conquerors through him who loved us. For I am sure that neither death, nor life, nor angels, nor principalities, nor things present, nor things to come, nor powers, nor height, nor depth, nor anything else in all creation, will be able to separate us from the love of God in Christ Jesus our Lord.

Trust that God will grant us what we ask for 'through our Lord Jesus Christ' means trust that what St. Paul says is true. Because in his mercy and goodness God the Father sent His Son Jesus Christ for the sake of our salvation and because Jesus Christ was raised from dead and is at the right hand of God interceding for us, we have a double guarantee 'through Jesus Christ' that nothing can separate us from God's love. We can therefore trust that God will grant us those things that we ask for when we pray the Lord's Prayer, provision for all our daily needs and protection from evil in this life and the life to come. It is on the basis of that trust that we say 'Amen', 'so be it.'

4.5   The Sacraments

The additional section on the Sacraments which was added to the Catechism in 1604 begins by stating that Christ has ordained two sacraments, Baptism and the Supper of the Lord.

As well as saying that Baptism and the Lord's Supper are the only two sacraments ordained by Christ, the Catechism also declares that they are 'generally necessary for salvation.' 'Generally' is used here in its normal sixteenth and seventeenth century sense of 'universally,' so what the Catechism is saying is that the sacraments are a necessary part of salvation for everyone. Christ did not ordain them as optional extras but as an integral part of the way that Christians receive salvation. That is why Christ gave commanded his followers to baptise all nations (Matthew 28:19) and to continue to celebrate the Lord's Supper (1 Corinthians 11:23-25). These are the means through which Christians are born again of water and the Spirit (John 3:5) and receive eternal life through feeding on the flesh of the Son of Man and drinking his blood (John 6:53).

In relation to Baptism the Catechism follows Matthew 28:19 in seeing the outward sign as baptism with water in the name of the Father, and of the Son, and of the Holy Spirit. The grace to which this points is a movement from being 'children of wrath' (Ephesians 2:3) to 'children of grace' (Galatians 3:26-4:7) involving a 'death unto sin, and a new birth unto righteousness' (Romans 6:1-11).

As we noted when looking at earlier sections of the Catechism, divine grace requires a human response and the response which is required in the case of Baptism is defined as repentance leading people to 'forsake sin' and faith involving steadfast belief in 'the promises of God, made to them in that Sacrament.' In the words of Robinson 'those who would thus pass from the death of sin into the life of righteousness must of necessity hate and renounce the ways of evil, and turn with trust to Him Who will not fail to meet and bless them in the appointed means of grace.'[26] The Biblical basis for this requirement of repentance and faith is Acts 2:38 and Mark 16:16.

In the opening section of the Catechism the promises made at Baptism involve not only repentance and faith, but also a commitment to 'keep God's holy will and commandments.' The question has therefore been raised as to why there is no equivalent to this third promise in this latter part of the Catechism. The most probable answer is that repentance and faith were both seen to involve a commitment to obedience to God and so the third promise is implied.

The requirement for repentance and faith leads to the obvious question about how children can be baptised when 'by reason of their tender age' they are not capable of either. To quote Colquhoun, the answer given by the Catechism is that the promises of repentance and faith:

> ...are made on their behalf by their godparents – here called their *sureties*, because in baptism they not only act as the mouthpiece of the child (as sponsors) but also give 'surety' or security that the child will be brought up in the Christian faith.[27]

---

[26] Robinson, *The Church Catechism Explained*, p 143.
[27] Colquhoun, *Catechism and Confirmation*, p 143.

Repeating a point made in its opening section, the Catechism adds that children are 'bound to perform' the promises made on their behalf 'when they come of age.' The view of the English Reformers was that it is when this happens that people 'receive baptism rightly' (Article XXVII) and enjoy the blessings which Baptism conveys. To quote Archbishop James Ussher:

> As Baptism administered to those of years is not effectual unless they believe, so we can make no comfortable use of our baptism administered in our infancy until we believe. All the promises of grace were in my Baptism estated unto me, and sealed up unto me on God's part; but then I come to have the profit and benefit of them when I come to understand what grant God in Baptism hath sealed unto me and actually lay hold of it by faith.[28]

The Catechism begins its account of the Lord's Supper by explaining that it was ordained 'for the continual remembrance of the sacrifice of the death of Christ, and of the benefits which we receive thereby.' The idea that the Lord's Supper was instituted for the purpose of remembrance is derived from St Paul's account of the Last Supper in 1 Corinthians 11:23-26:

> For I received from the Lord what I also delivered to you, that the Lord Jesus on the night when he was betrayed took bread, and when he had given thanks, he broke it, and said, 'This is my body which is for you. Do this in remembrance of me.' In the same way also the cup, after supper, saying, 'This cup is the new covenant in my blood. Do this, as often as you drink it, in remembrance of me.' For as often as you eat this bread and drink the cup, you proclaim the Lord's death until he comes.

Robinson argues that 'remembering' the death of Christ could mean remembering it before God in the sense of 'presenting before God the one sacrifice once offered as the one and only hope upon which we rest our hopes of salvation' or remembering it before the world in the sense of testifying 'before all to the reality of redemption.'[29] However, the most likely meaning of remembering in the Catechism is our remembering what Christ has done for us. As Alexander Nowell put it, the 'use' of the Lord's Supper is 'to celebrate and retain continually a

---

[28] Quoted in Griffith Thomas, *The Catholic Faith*, pp 111-12.
[29] Robinson, *The Church Catechism Explained*, p 148.

thankful remembrance of our Lord's death and of the most singular benefit which we have received thereby.'[30]

The Catechism next goes on to explain the outward and inward elements of the Lord's Supper.

The outward sign is 'Bread and Wine, which the Lord hath commanded to be received.' The words 'which the Lord hath commanded to be received' point back to the words of Christ in St Matthew's account of the Last Supper 'take, eat; this is my body' and 'drink of it, all of you' (Matthew 26:26-27) and the point that is being made, over against the theology of the Middle Ages and the Counter-Reformation, is that the Christ's intention was that both elements were to be received (rather than the laity being given the bread only) and that the elements were to be consumed rather than adored.[31]

The inward reality is the 'Body and Blood of Christ, which are verily and indeed taken and received by the faithful in the Lord's Supper.' The English Reformers whose views are reflected here believed on the basis of 1 Corinthians 10:16 that there is a real reception of the body and blood of Christ in the Lord's Supper. In the words of Article XXVIII, 'to such as rightly, worthily and with faith, receive the same, the Bread which we break is a partaking of the Body of Christ; and likewise the Cup of Blessing is a partaking of the Blood of Christ.'

However, they also believed that the body and blood of Christ are *only* received by the faithful. In the words of Article XXIX:

> The wicked and such as be void of a lively faith, although they do carnally and visibly press with their teeth (as S. Augustine saith) the sacrament of the body and blood of Christ, yet in no wise are they partakers of Christ, but rather to their condemnation do eat and drink the sign or sacrament of so great a thing.

According to the Catechism, the benefit when we do receive with faith is 'The strengthening and refreshing of our souls by the Body and Blood of Christ, as our bodies are by the Bread and Wine.' In the words of Colquhoun:

> The teaching of the Catechism here is twofold: (a) that nourishment is as surely needed by the soul as by the body; and that (b) the

---

[30] Corrie (ed) *Nowell's Catechism*, p 212.
[31] See Articles XXVIII and XXX.

> Holy Communion is one of the divinely appointed means by which that need is met. The soul of the Christian is fed by Christ's body and blood in the sacrament as truly as is his body by the bread and wine; and so he finds both strength and refreshment.[32]

The biblical basis for belief in this kind of spiritual feeding is the words of Jesus in John 6:54-58:

> He who eats my flesh and drinks my blood has eternal life, and I will raise him up at the last day. For my flesh is food indeed, and my blood is drink indeed. He who eats my flesh and drinks my blood abides in me, and I in him. As the living Father sent me, and I live because of the Father, so he who eats me will live because of me. This is the bread which came down from heaven, not such as the fathers ate and died; he who eats this bread will live for ever.

The Catechism concludes its teaching about the Lord's Supper with an explanation of what is required in order for people to receive the sacrament with faith and avoid eating and drinking the elements in a way that brings upon them the condemnation about which St Paul warns in 1 Corinthians 11:27-32. What is needed, it declares, is for people to examine themselves to see whether: 'they repent them truly of their former sins, steadfastly purposing to lead a new life; have a lively faith in God's mercy through Christ, with a thankful remembrance of his death; and be in charity with all men.'

---

[32] Colquhoun, *Catechism and Confirmation*, p 151.

5 The continuing value of the Catechism

As an element of the *Book of Common Prayer,* the Catechism forms part of the 'historic formularies' that together with the Bible, the teaching of the Fathers, and the Creeds constitute the basis for the theology and practice of the Church of England (see Canons A5 and C15). It follows that the teaching of the Catechism still has theological authority within the Church of England. It declares what the Church of England believes. However, its value is not restricted to its formal theological authority.

In his classic seventeenth century account of Anglican pastoral ministry, the *Country Parson,* George Herbert explains that the country parson will compile the theological resources he needs for his ministry on the basis of 'the Church Catechism, to which all divinity may easily be reduced.' What Herbert means by these words is that if we ask what theology is fundamentally about, the answer is that it is about those matters that are covered in the Catechism.

Theology is the study of God and his relationship with the human race. What we need to know from such study is who God is, what He has done for us and how we should respond to this; what we should believe, how we should behave, how we should pray, what the sacraments are and how we may receive them with spiritual benefit. On all these matters the Catechism provides us with clear, concise and biblically based teaching that draws on the insights of the theological renewal that took place at the Reformation. It is because this is the case that the Catechism still has value today.

The Catechism does not tell us everything that we may want to know theologically, but it tells us those things that we most need to know and it does so succinctly and truthfully. In the words of Colquhoun, 'the value of the Church Catechism is that it is concise and comprehensive, simple and scriptural. It adheres firmly to the essential facts of the Christian religion and refuses to get side-tracked on secondary issues.'[1]

---

[1] Colquhoun, *Catechism and Confirmation,* p 15.

If everyone knew and believed the teaching contained in the Catechism and acted upon it there would be a transformation in the life of the Church and of society.[2]

There are now other forms of Anglican catechetical material available (see Appendix B). However, it is arguable that these are not as useful as the Catechism when it comes to providing a basic introduction to the Christian faith. This is either because they are not as theologically reliable as the Catechism, or because they lack its brevity and clarity, or both.

It follows from this that there is a strong case for returning to the Catechism as a basis for teaching the fundamentals of the Christian faith in basics groups and confirmation classes. It is short enough to be learned by heart and this remains an invaluable way of imprinting basic Christian truth in our hearts and minds.

In the same way that the Church of Finland has recently produced catechetical material based on Luther's Small Catechism,[3] the Church of England (or groups within it) could and should produce catechetical material based round the Prayer Book Catechism. Using the Catechism as a basis for catechetical instruction has worked well for the Church of England in the past and there seems to be no reason why it should not continue to work well for the Church of England in the present.

It is true that some of the language in the Catechism is now dated, such as the use of the word 'ghostly' when we would say 'spiritual' and the use of the word 'generally' when we would say 'universally'. However, there are not that many dated words used in the Catechism and those that do exist can easily be explained when the meaning of the Catechism is expounded.

It is also true that the baptismal promises referred to in the Catechism no longer correspond to the promises that are normally made at Baptism since the promises made in the *Common Worship* baptism services are different from those in the *Book of Common Prayer*. However, this too is not an insuperable difficulty. The point that needs to be made is that the promises referred to in the Catechism are promises which flow from the nature of Baptism itself. It follows that everyone who has been baptised should be seeking to live out these

---

[2] For the transformation that would take place in society see Appendix C.
[3] *Catechism*, (Helsinki: Edita, 2001).

promises, regardless of the specific words that were used when they were baptised.

Finally, the Catechism is based on the assumption that the individual being catechised is a child who was baptised as an infant whereas as increasing proportion of baptisms that take place today are of adults. However, this does not negate the value of the Catechism because it is just as applicable to an adult as to a child. To quote Bishop Ken again:

> It is a great error to think that the Catechism was meant for children only: for all Christians are equally concerned in those saving truths which are there taught; and the doctrine delivered in the Catechism is as proper for the study and as necessary for the salvation of a great doctor as of a weak Christian or a young child.[4]

---

[4] Quoted in Colquhoun, *Catechism and Confirmation*, p 16.

Appendix A   The Catechism of 1549

A CATECHISME,

THAT IS TO SAY,

AN INSTRUCCION TO BEE LEARNED OF EVERY CHILDE, BEFORE HE BE BROUGHT TO BE CONFIRMED OF THE BUSHOP.

Question. What is your name?

Aunswere. N or M.

Question. Who gave you this name?

Aunswere. My Godfathers and Godmothers in my Baptisme, wherein I was made a member of Christe, the childe of God, and inheritour of the kingdome of heaven.

Question. What did your Godfathers and Godmothers then for you?

Aunswere. They did promise and vowe three thinges in my name. First, that I should forsake the devil and all his workes and pompes, the vanities of the wicked worlde, and all the sinne full lustes of the fleshe. Secondly, that I should beleve all the articles of the Christian fayth. And thirdly, that I should kepe Goddes holy will and commaundementes and walke in the same al the daies of my life.

Question. Dooest thou not thinke that thou arte bound to beleve, and to doe as they have promised for thee?

Aunswere. Yes verely. And by Gods helpe so I wil. And I hartily thanke our heavenly father, that he hath called me to thys state of salvacion, through Jesus Christe our Saveour And I pray God to geve me hys grace, that I may continue in the same unto my lives ende.

Question. Rehearse the articles of thy beliefe.

Aunswere. I beleve in God the father almightie, maker of heaven and earth. And in Jesus Christ his only sonne our lord. Whiche was conceived by the holy gost, borne of the virgin Marie. Suffered under Ponce Pilate, was crucified, dead, and buried, he descended into hel. The third day he rose agayn from the dead. He ascended into heaven, and sitteth on the right hande of God the father almightie. From thence shal he come to judge the quicke and the dead. I beleve in the holy goste. The holye catholike church. The communion of saintes. The forgevenes of sinnes. The resurreccion of the bodie. And the lyfe everlasting. Amen.

Question. What dooest thou chiefely learne in these articles of thy beliefe?

Aunswere. Firste, I learne to beleve in God the father, who hath made me and all the worlde.

Secondely, in God the sonne who hath redemed me and all mankinde.

Thirdly, in god the holy goste, who sanctifyeth me and all the electe people of god.

Question. You sayde that your Godfathers and Godmothers dyd promyse for you that ye should kepe Goddes commaundementes. Tell me how many there bee.

Aunswere. Tenne.

Question. Whiche be they?

Aunswere. I. Thou shalte have none other Gods but me.

II. Thou shalte not make to thyselfe anye graven image, nor the likenesse of any thyng that is in heaven above, or in the earth beneath, nor in the water under the earth: thou shalt not bowe downe to them, nor wurship them.

III. Thou shalt not take the name of the lord thy God in vayne.

IV. Remember that thou kepe holy the Sabboth day.

V. Honor thy father and thy mother.

VI. Thou shalt doe no murdre.

VII. Thou shalt not commit adultry.

VIII. Thou shalt not steale.

IX. Thou shalt not beare false witnes against thy neighbour.

X. Thou shalt not covet thy neighbours wife, nor his servaunt, nor his mayde, nor his Oxe, nor his Asse, nor any thing that is his.

Question. What dooest thou chiefely leame by these commaundemente?

Aunswere. I learne two thinges: My duetie towardes god, and my duetie towardes my neighbour.

Question. What is thy duetie towardes god?

Aunswere. My duetie towardes God is, to beleve in him. To feare him. And to love him with al my hart, with al my mind, with al my soule, and with all my strength. To wurship him. To geve him thankes. To put my whole truste in hym. To call upon him. To honor his holy name and his word, and to serve him truely all the daies of my life.

Question. What is thy dutie towardes thy neighboure?

Answere. My duetie towardes my neighbour is, to love hym as myselfe. And to do to al men as I would they should do to me. To love, honour, and succoure my father and mother. To honour and obey the kyng and his ministers. To submitte myselfe to all my governours, teachers, spirituall pastours, and maisters. To ordre myselfe lowlye and reverentelye to al my betters. To hurte no bodie by woorde nor dede. To bee true and just in al my dealing. To beare no malice nor hatred in my heart. To kepe my handes from picking and stealing, and my tongue from evill speaking, liyng, and slaundring. To kepe my bodie in temperaunce, sobreness, and chastitie. Not to covet nor desire other mennes goodes. But learne and laboure truely to geate my owne living, and to doe my duetie in that state of life: unto which it shal please God to cal me.

Question. My good sonne, knowe this, that thou arte not hable to do these thinges of thyself, nor to walke in the commaundementes of God and to serve him, without his speciall grace, which thou muste leame at all times to cal for by diligent prayer. Leat me heare therfore if thou canst say the Lordes prayer.

Answere. Our father whiche art in heaven, halowed bee thy name. Thy kyngdome come. Thy wil bee done in earth as it is in heaven. Geve us this day our dailye breade. And forgene us our trespasses, as we forgeve them that trespasse againste us. And leade us not into temptacion, but deliver us from evil. Amen.

Question. What desireste thou of God in this prayer?

Answere. I desire my lord god our heavenly father, who is the gever of al goodnes, to send his grace unto me, and to all people, that we may wurship him, serve hym, and obey him, as we ought to doe. And I praye unto God, that he will sende us al thynges that be nedeful both for our soules and bodies: And that he wil bee mercifull unto us, and forgeve us our sinnes: And that it will please him to save and defende us in al daungers gostly [=spiritually] and bodily: And that he wil kepe us from al sinne and wickednes, and from our gostly enemye, and from everlastyng death. And this I truste he wil doe of his mercie and goodnes, through our lorde Jesu Christe. And therefore I say, Amen. So be it.

¶ So soone as the children can say in their mother tongue tharticles of the faith, the lordes praier, the ten commaundementes, and also can aunswere to such questions of this short Cathechisme as the Bushop (or suche as he shall appointe) shal by hys discrecion appose them in: then shall they bee brought to the Bushop by one that shalbee his godfather or godmother, that everye childe maye have a wittenesse of hys confirmacion.

¶ And the Bushop shal confirme them on this wyse.[1]

---

[1] Text in http://justus.anglican.org/resources/bcp/1549/Confirmation_1549.htm

Appendix B   Alternative Anglican catechetical material

The Revised Catechism (1962)

For three hundred years the Catechism remained the only authorised catechism in the Church of England. In 1962 however, the *Revised Catechism* was authorised for use by the Convocations of Canterbury and York.

This was a revision of the Catechism and its purpose was:

1. To enlarge the scope of the *Prayer Book* Catechism by adding material on the Church, the Means of Grace, the Bible, Christian Duty, and the Christian Hope.

2. To modernize the language and to make it more appropriate to present social conditions.[1]

The *Revised Catechism* follows the basic pattern of the Catechism and its question and answer format and contains a lot of useful catechetical material on topics that are not covered in the Catechism such as the Church and the Bible. However, it is much less concise than the *Prayer Book* Catechism (61 questions and answers as against 25) which makes it less easy for people to memorize. It also contains no exposition of the Lord's Prayer and some of its teaching is problematic.

It blurs the distinction between the Gospel sacraments of Baptism and Holy Communion and what it calls 'other sacramental ministries of grace' (confirmation, ordination, holy matrimony, the ministry of absolution and the ministry of healing.)[2] It says that Baptism and Holy Communion are 'needed by all for fullness of life' rather than 'necessary for salvation.'[3] It says that at confirmation 'the Holy Spirit is received to complete what he began in Baptism'[4] wrongly suggesting that what happened at Baptism was somehow incomplete. Finally, its account of the last judgment says that God 'will condemn and destroy all that is evil, and bring his servants into the joy of their Lord.'[5] This is

---

[1] *The Revised Catechism*, (London: SPCK, 1974), p iii.
[2] *The Revised Catechism*, p 13.
[3] *The Revised Catechism*, p 13.
[4] *The Revised Catechism*, p 15.
[5] *The Revised Catechism*, p 19.

true as far as it goes, but it does not say anything specifically about the fate of the lost.

The best way to use the *Revised Catechism* is to make selective use of it to supplement the Catechism.

Pilgrim

Pilgrim is a new set of catechetical resources from the Church of England designed to supplement the *Revised Catechism*. The entire set of resources has not yet been published, but when it is available in 2015 it will consist of two sets of four short books. The books in the 'Follow' set will provide material for 'those who are enquirers and very new to the faith' covering 'Turning to Christ,' 'The Lord's Prayer,' 'The Commandments' and 'The Beatitudes.' The books in the 'Grow' set will provide material 'designed for those who want to go further and learn more' covering 'The Creeds,' 'The Eucharist,' 'The Bible' and 'Church and Kingdom.'

The *Pilgrim* material has a similar format to other contemporary basics courses such as *Alpha*, *Emmaus* and *Christianity Explored*. What each book offers is material for six study group sessions consisting of prayers, a passage from Scripture, a reflection on that passage and wider theological issues related to it, questions for group discussion and additional quotations from a range of writers ancient and modern. Additional film resources are also available from the Pilgrim web site.

The material that has been published so far is of high quality and much of the content is very helpful. However, the format of the material means that it does not offer any form of concise and memorable summary of the basics of the Christian faith. The idea seems to be that the *Revised Catechism* will continue to offer this in the slightly updated form offered in the 'Follow' Leaders Guide.[6] In addition the material published so far has some important gaps.

Thus in the 'Turning to Christ' material in the 'Follow' set we are told that in Christ 'God is one with us'[7] but these is no clear explanation of the deity of Christ or what it means to say that He is both God and Man. Likewise there is mention of the doctrine of the Trinity and that

---

[6] *Pilgrim, Follow Leaders Guide*, (London: Church House Publishing, 2013), pp 71-84.
[7] *Pilgrim, Turning to Christ*, (London: Church House Publishing, 2013), p 22.

Christ's death was a sacrifice for the sins of the world, but no explanation of either.[8] Finally, in the session on renouncing evil, the nature of evil is discussed without any mention of the Devil.[9]

What all this means is that *Pilgrim* does not replace the Catechism as a basic summary of the Christian faith and although it contains much useful material anyone using it will need to be aware of the gaps it contains and to think how these can be covered.

To be a Christian

In January 2014 The Anglican Church in North America published its new catechism entitled 'To be a Christian.' Using a traditional question and answer format this catechism, produced by a team led by J I Packer, covers the basics of salvation, the Apostles Creed and the life of faith, the Christian life and the Lord's Prayer and the Ten Commandments and obedience to Christ. It also has prayers to accompany the catechism, a rite for the admission of catechumens, the texts of the Apostles, Nicene and Athanasian Creeds and a discussion document on the development of an Anglican Catechumenate.

The catechism itself is extraordinarily comprehensive and the questions and answers it contains are clear, concise and biblically based. For example, the answer to the question 'Who is God?' is 'God is one divine being eternally existing in three Divine Persons: the Father, the Son and the Holy Spirit. This is the Holy Trinity. (Matthew 3:16 and 17, 28:19)' and the answer to the question 'Who is Jesus Christ?' is 'Jesus Christ is the eternal Word and Son of God, the second person of the Holy Trinity. He took on flesh to be the Saviour and Redeemer of the world, the only Mediator between God and fallen mankind. (1 Timothy 2:5, John 1:14, 14:6, 1 Peter 1:18-19)'.

Because of these strengths it provides a wonderful theological resource. However, it is sixty four pages long and contains 345 questions and therefore is best used selectively rather than being given to people complete as a basic course of Christian instruction.

---

[8] *Pilgrim, Turning to Christ*, pp 41 and 48.
[9] *Pilgrim, Turning to Christ*, pp 55-63.

Appendix C   The social significance of the teaching of the Catechism about our duty towards our neighbour.

The potential significance of the teaching of the Catechism for the wellbeing of society was explained by the Victorian writer Sir James Fitzjames Stephens in his *History of the Criminal Law of England* in 1883:

> The criminal law may be described with truth as the expansion of the second table of the Ten Commandments. The statement of the Catechism of the positive duties of man to man corresponds step by step with prohibitions of a Criminal Code. Those who honour and obey the Queen will not commit high treason or other political offences. Those who honour and obey in their due order and degree those who are put in authority under the Queen will not attempt to pervert the course of justice, nor will they disobey lawful commands, or violate the provisions of acts of parliament, or be guilty of corrupt practices with regard to public officers or in the discharge of powers confided to them by law.
>
> Those who hurt nobody by word will not commit libel or threaten injury to person, property, or reputation, nor will they lie in courts of justice or elsewhere, but will keep their tongues from evil-speaking, lying and slandering. Those who hurt nobody by deed will not commit murder or administer poison, wound or assault others, or burn their houses, or maliciously injure their property.
>
> Those who keep their hands from picking stealing will commit neither thefts, nor fraudulent breaches of trust, nor forgery, nor will they pass bad money. Those who keep their bodies in temperance, soberness and chastity, will not only not commit rape and other offences even more abominable, but will avoid the causes that lead to the commission of nearly all crimes.
>
> Those who learn and labour truly to get their own living will not be disorderly persons, cheats, imposters, rogues or vagabonds, and will at all events have taken a long step towards doing their duty in the state of life to which it has pleased God to call them.[1]

---

[1] Quoted in Robinson, *The Church Catechism Explained*, pp 161-162.

If you have enjoyed this book, you might like to consider

- *supporting the work of the Latimer Trust*
- *reading more of our publications*
- *recommending them to others*

See www.latimertrust.org for more information.

Latimer Publications

Latimer Studies

LS 01	The Evangelical Anglican Identity Problem	Jim Packer
LS 02	The ASB Rite A Communion: A Way Forward	Roger Beckwith
LS 03	The Doctrine of Justification in the Church of England	Robin Leaver
LS 04	Justification Today: The Roman Catholic and Anglican Debate	R. G. England
LS 05/06	Homosexuals in the Christian Fellowship	David Atkinson
LS 07	Nationhood: A Christian Perspective	O. R. Johnston
LS 08	Evangelical Anglican Identity: Problems and Prospects	Tom Wright
LS 09	Confessing the Faith in the Church of England Today	Roger Beckwith
LS 10	A Kind of Noah's Ark? The Anglican Commitment to Comprehensiveness	Jim Packer
LS 11	Sickness and Healing in the Church	Donald Allister
LS 12	Rome and Reformation Today: How Luther Speaks to the New Situation	James Atkinson
LS 13	Music as Preaching: Bach, Passions and Music in Worship	Robin Leaver
LS 14	Jesus Through Other Eyes: Christology in a Multi-faith Context	Christopher Lamb
LS 15	Church and State Under God	James Atkinson,
LS 16	Language and Liturgy	Gerald Bray, Steve Wilcockson, Robin Leaver
LS 17	Christianity and Judaism: New Understanding, New Relationship	James Atkinson
LS 18	Sacraments and Ministry in Ecumenical Perspective	Gerald Bray
LS 19	The Functions of a National Church	Max Warren
LS 20/21	The Thirty-Nine Articles: Their Place and Use Today	Jim Packer, Roger Beckwith
LS 22	How We Got Our Prayer Book	T.W. Drury, Roger Beckwith
LS 23/24	Creation or Evolution: a False Antithesis?	Mike Poole, Gordon Wenham
LS 25	Christianity and the Craft	Gerard Moate
LS 26	ARCIC II and Justification	Alister McGrath
LS 27	The Challenge of the Housechurches	Tony Higton, Gilbert Kirby
LS 28	Communion for Children? The Current Debate	A. A. Langdon
LS 29/30	Theological Politics	Nigel Biggar
LS 31	Eucharistic Consecration in the First Four Centuries and its Implications for Liturgical Reform	Nigel Scotland
LS 32	A Christian Theological Language	Gerald Bray
LS 33	Mission in Unity: The Bible and Missionary Structures	Duncan McMann
LS 34	Stewards of Creation: Environmentalism in the Light of Biblical Teaching	Lawrence Osborn
LS 35/36	Mission and Evangelism in Recent Thinking: 1974-1986	Robert Bashford
LS 37	Future Patterns of Episcopacy: Reflections in Retirement	Stuart Blanch
LS 38	Christian Character: Jeremy Taylor and Christian Ethics Today	David Scott
LS 39	Islam: Towards a Christian Assessment	Hugh Goddard
LS 40	Liberal Catholicism: Charles Gore and the Question of Authority	G. F. Grimes
LS 41/42	The Christian Message in a Multi-faith Society	Colin Chapman
LS 43	The Way of Holiness 1: Principles	D. A. Ousley
LS 44/45	The Lambeth Articles	V. C. Miller
LS 46	The Way of Holiness 2: Issues	D. A. Ousley

Latimer Publications

LS 47	Building Multi-Racial Churches	John Root
LS 48	Episcopal Oversight: A Case for Reform	David Holloway
LS 49	Euthanasia: A Christian Evaluation	Henk Jochemsen
LS 50/51	The Rough Places Plain: AEA 1995	
LS 52	A Critique of Spirituality	John Pearce
LS 53/54	The Toronto Blessing	Martyn Percy
LS 55	The Theology of Rowan Williams	Garry Williams
LS 56/57	Reforming Forwards? The Process of Reception and the Consecration of Woman as Bishops	Peter Toon
LS 58	The Oath of Canonical Obedience	Gerald Bray
LS 59	The Parish System: The Same Yesterday, Today And For Ever?	Mark Burkill
LS 60	'I Absolve You': Private Confession and the Church of England	Andrew Atherstone
LS 61	The Water and the Wine: A Contribution to the Debate on Children and Holy Communion	Roger Beckwith, Andrew Daunton-Fear
LS 62	Must God Punish Sin?	Ben Cooper
LS 63	Too Big For Words? The Transcendence of God and Finite Human Speech	Mark D. Thompson
LS 64	A Step Too Far: An Evangelical Critique of Christian Mysticism	Marian Raikes
LS 65	The New Testament and Slavery: Approaches and Implications	Mark Meynell
LS 66	The Tragedy of 1662: The Ejection and Persecution of the Puritans	Lee Gatiss
LS 67	Heresy, Schism & Apostasy	Gerald Bray
LS 68	Paul in 3D: Preaching Paul as Pastor, Story-teller and Sage	Ben Cooper
LS69	Christianity and the Tolerance of Liberalism: J.Gresham Machen and the Presbyterian Controversy of 1922-1937	Lee Gatiss
LS70	An Anglican Evangelical Identity Crisis: The Churchman–Anvil Affair of 1981-4	Andrew Atherstone
LS71	Empty and Evil: The worship of other faiths in 1 Corinthians 8-10 and today	Rohintan Mody
LS72	To Plough or to Preach: Mission Strategies in New Zealand during the 1820s	Malcolm Falloon
LS73	Plastic People: How Queer Theory is changing us	Peter Sanlon
LS74	Deification and Union with Christ: Salvation in Orthodox and Reformed thought	Slavko Eždenci
LS75	As It Is Written: Interpreting the Bible with Boldness	Benjamin Sargent
LS76	Light From Dark Ages? An Evangelical Critique of Celtic Spirituality	Marian Raikes
LS77	The Ethics of Usury	Ben Cooper
LS78	For Us and For Our Salvation: 'Limited Atonement' in the Bible, Doctrine, History and Ministry	Lee Gatiss
LS79	Positive Complementarianism: The Key Biblical Texts	Ben Cooper

Latimer Publications

Anglican Foundations Series

FWC	*The Faith We Confess: An Exposition of the 39 Articles*	Gerald Bray
AF02	*The 'Very Pure Word of God': The Book of Common Prayer as a Model of Biblical Liturgy*	Peter Adam
AF03	*Dearly Beloved: Building God's People Through Morning and Evening Prayer*	Mark Burkill
AF04	*Day by Day: The Rhythm of the Bible in the Book of Common Prayer*	Benjamin Sargent
AF05	*The Supper: Cranmer and Communion*	Nigel Scotland
AF06	*A Fruitful Exhortation: A Guide to the Homilies*	Gerald Bray
AF07	*Instruction in the Way: A Guide to the Catechism in the Book of Common Prayer*	Martin Davie
AF08	*Till Death us do Part: "The Solemnization of Matrimony" in the Book of Common Prayer*	Simon Vibert

Latimer Books

GGC	*God, Gays and the Church: Human Sexuality and Experience in Christian Thinking*	eds. Lisa Nolland, Chris Sugden, Sarah Finch
WTL	*The Way, the Truth and the Life: Theological Resources for a Pilgrimage to a Global Anglican Future*	eds. Vinay Samuel, Chris Sugden, Sarah Finch
AEID	*Anglican Evangelical Identity – Yesterday and Today*	J.I.Packer, N.T.Wright
IB	*The Anglican Evangelical Doctrine of Infant Baptism*	John Stott, Alec Motyer
BF	*Being Faithful: The Shape of Historic Anglicanism Today*	Theological Resource Group of GAFCON
TPG	*The True Profession of the Gospel: Augustus Toplady and Reclaiming our Reformed Foundations*	Lee Gatiss
SG	*Shadow Gospel: Rowan Williams and the Anglican Communion Crisis*	Charles Raven
TTB	*Translating the Bible: From Willliam Tyndale to King James*	Gerald Bray
PWS	*Pilgrims, Warriors, and Servants: Puritan Wisdom for Today's Church*	ed. Lee Gatiss
PPA	*Preachers, Pastors, and Ambassadors: Puritan Wisdom for Today's Church*	ed. Lee Gatiss
CWP	*The Church, Women Bishops and Provision: The Integrity of Orthodox Objections to the Proposed Legislation Allowing Women Bishops*	
TSF	*The Truth Shall Set You Free: Global Anglicans in the 21st Century*	ed. Charles Raven
LMM	*Launching Marsden's Mission: The Beginnings of the Church Missionary Society in New Zealand, viewed from New South Wales*	eds. Peter G Bolt, David B. Pettett

Latimer Publications

Latimer Briefings

LB01	The Church of England: What it is, and what it stands for	R. T. Beckwith
LB02	Praying with Understanding: Explanations of Words and Passages in the Book of Common Prayer	R. T. Beckwith
LB03	The Failure of the Church of England? The Church, the Nation and the Anglican Communion	A. Pollard
LB04	Towards a Heritage Renewed	H.R.M. Craig
LB05	Christ's Gospel to the Nations: The Heart & Mind of Evangelicalism Past, Present & Future	Peter Jensen
LB06	Passion for the Gospel: Hugh Latimer (1485–1555) Then and Now. A commemorative lecture to mark the 450th anniversary of his martyrdom in Oxford	A. McGrath
LB07	Truth and Unity in Christian Fellowship	Michael Nazir-Ali
LB08	Unworthy Ministers: Donatism and Discipline Today	Mark Burkill
LB09	Witnessing to Western Muslims: A Worldview Approach to Sharing Faith	Richard Shumack
LB10	Scarf or Stole at Ordination? A Plea for the Evangelical Conscience	Andrew Atherstone
LB11	How to Write a Theology Essay	Michael P. Jensen
LB12	Preaching: A Guidebook for Beginners	Allan Chapple
LB13	Justification by Faith: Orientating the Church's teaching and practice to Christ (Toon Lecture 1)	Michael Nazir-Ali
LB14	"Remember Your Leaders": Principles and Priorities for Leaders from Hebrews 13	Wallace Benn
LB15	How the Anglican Communion came to be and where it is going	Michael Nazir-Ali
LB16	Divine Allurement: Cranmer's Comfortable Words	Ashley Null